SR

Books are to be returned on or before
the last date below.

- 6 DEC 2012 3 0 SEP 2016

2 6 MAR 2013
2 3 APR 2013

2 9 MAY 2013
2 1 AUG 2013

1 0 JAN 2014

2 7 FEB 2014
2 7 MAY 2014

- 9 SEP 2014
1 9 DEC 2014
2 2 APR 2015

- 8 DEC 2015
- 7 JAN 2016
2 8 JUN 2016

With thanks to Hannah Frew.

Bloodsucking for Beginners

by Anne Rooney
www.annerooney.co.uk

Published by Ransom Publishing Ltd.
Radley House, 8 St. Cross Road, Winchester, Hants.
SO23 9HX, UK
www.ransom.co.uk

ISBN   978 184167 303 5

First published in 2012

Bloodsucking
for
Beginners

ANNE ROONEY

Ransom

Contents

Welcome

Shroud-eater, vampire, upir, revenant, undead, bloodsucker ...

We have been called all these names – and more. Whatever name is current in your location and time, welcome!

So, now you're a vampire. It will take a bit of getting used to. Sometimes you will be angry, sometimes you will be resentful – and sometimes you will be excited. Try to take it all in your stride.

Eventually you will feel at peace with your new self. And you have all the time in the world for that to happen.

In the meantime, this guide will help you to get to grips with the day-to-day business of being a vampire.

It will cover all you need to know, including:

- Your vampire body

- The A – Z of daily life as a vampire

- Dealing with the NV ('non-vampire') world

- Living forever

- Vampire science

- Vampire fact and fiction

- Vampire history

- Vampire FAQs.

So, let's begin.

Your Vampire Body

Vampirism is a medical condition.

It has effects on your body (*physical effects*) and on your mind (*psychological effects*).

You may find these strange at first, and hard to get used to. Don't worry: you will soon adapt.

What seems odd and unnatural now will seem perfectly normal in a hundred years or so. In fact, some vampires forget what it was like to be any other way.

You will have noticed some of these changes in yourself already; others will become obvious over time.

Physical Effects

Urgent hunger for blood

Your body has an increased need for iron, now you are a vampire. The need for iron produces a hunger for it that is manic if not controlled by drugs.

Blood is rich in iron. The urge to feast on blood will feel very strong. Do not be alarmed: this is normal.

Lack of normal hunger

You no longer need to eat ordinary food and, indeed, you cannot easily digest it.

Normal food may make you vomit.

Reduced heartbeat

Your heartbeat may be almost undetectable, especially when you are asleep or in a coma. You may appear to an observer to be dead.

As a result of your slower heartbeat, you will have low blood pressure and you will not bleed if injured.

Pale skin

Your reduced heartbeat means that blood tends to pool at the bottom of your body, so your face and arms look whiter than normal.

If you are lying down, blood pools at your back, just as it does in a dead body.

Reduced breathing

Your breathing may be almost undetectable, especially when you are asleep or in a coma. As a result, you can stay under water for a long time without drowning.

Increased healing capacity

If you are injured or unwell, you will get better much more quickly than an NV (non-vampire).

You will recover from injuries that would be fatal to an NV.

This has given rise to the belief that vampires can only be killed by decapitation, staking, burning or a bullet through the heart.

In fact, a bullet through the heart is not always fatal, and inefficient staking can cause a nasty wound — but not death.

Perfect skin

Improved oxygen transport by your blood means that small injuries and spots heal quickly, so your skin will look better than it did before.

Living forever

It is not strictly true that vampires live forever, but we do live for a very long time.

The oldest known vampire is 850 years old. Others claim to be older than this, but have not been able to prove their age.

Psychological Effects

Arithmomania

One of the stranger psychological features of vampirism is an obsessive desire to count small objects, such as grains of rice or sand.

Religious aversion

If you had a religion prior to becoming a vampire, the signs and symbols of that religion will now be repellent to you.

This is another psychological effect, but it is so powerful that the shock of contact with the symbols of your previous religion might even cause physical injury. The symbol most often associated with this effect is the crucifix.

Aversion to bright light

It is not true that vampires cannot go out in daytime, but you might find bright sunlight hurts your eyes or causes headaches or even migraines.

Some artificial light has the same effect. Effects vary between individuals.

Depression

At first, it can be difficult to come to terms with missing out on activities you previously enjoyed, such as eating good food with your family or going to the beach.

Many new vampires find the idea of living long beyond the deaths of their loved ones particularly hard to accept.

Depression is normal. It may last up to 100 years, but taking proVamp regularly will help to keep it under control.

A – Z of Life
as a Vampire

As you can imagine, the effects of being a vampire can make everyday life amongst non-vampires difficult.

In your first years as a vampire, while your family is still alive, this will cause some problems for you.

You don't need to eat normal food – yet it is difficult to avoid eating in public. You age very slowly, and that makes people suspicious if you stay in the same place too long. You don't bleed properly if you are cut, but you might fall greedily on someone else who is cut and bleeding.

All these features make it very difficult to live normally amongst NVs.

Ageing

You will age very slowly. This means that you can't stay in the same place for a very long time because people will notice. You will need to move to a different area every 10 –15 years.

You can't become famous, and you will have to fall out with your family.

Arithmomania

see *Counting*.

Beheading

Beheading is one of the few methods of killing vampires that always works. Avoid situations in which you might be beheaded.

Biting

DO NOT BITE PEOPLE. This is very important. If you once get a taste for human blood, you will find it difficult to give it up. Anyone you bite might become a vampire.

Bleeding

Not bleeding when you are injured attracts attention. If you hurt yourself, hide the injury as well as you can.

Do not let pain get the better of you – hiding your non-bleeding wound is more important than pain relief.

Do not under any circumstances agree to give blood. If pressed to give blood, say you have malaria.

Burning

In some cases, vampires have been burned to death. More often, they are hurt and scarred.

Children

Children who become vampires in an NV family must, sadly, be kidnapped to avoid their families realising they do not age normally.

These children are brought up by loving vampire foster-families.

Chunking

A little-known and rarely used method of killing vampires is to cut them into small pieces. This is called *chunking*.

Coffin

It is not necessary to sleep in a coffin. Some vampires choose to do this. They tend to be older vampires who have lived through times when NVs hunted down vampires and destroyed them.

Counting

If small objects are dropped or sprinkled near you, you will feel an uncontrollable urge to count them. This is called 'arithmomania'. It is a very inconvenient effect of vampirehood.

You will need to avoid situations in which small objects are thrown, such as weddings.

Decapitation

see *Beheading*.

Doctors

If you are ill, you must see a vampire doctor. Your mentor will put you in touch with your nearest vampire doctor.

Vampire doctors are not all vampires themselves, but they are always under our control. They know about the vampire body and how to treat you.

Drinking

You can drink most things normally.

Adult vampires may drink alcohol. Don't drink too much, as its effects are greater than for an NV. This is a result of the more efficient working of your body.

Do not drink milk on its own or in milkshakes or hot chocolate. It will make you sick.

Drugs

Please don't take any drugs unless you have been given them by a vampire doctor. The effects of illegal drugs and some medical drugs are different on vampires.

Eating

You are able to eat raw or nearly-raw meat. You can eat cooked meat but it will feel heavy in your stomach, so eating too much will make you feel unwell.

You can eat small quantities of vegetables and salad, but very little stodgy food such as rice, pasta, bread and potatoes.

You might be sick after eating normal food in any quantity. Your body is now very efficient and can take all the nutrients it needs from a small quantity of food.

You will find that people press you to eat. You will have to develop strategies for dealing with this.

If you are young, people might suspect you have an eating disorder and then they will watch you very closely, making your life difficult.

The easiest and most successful way of managing food problems is to say that you have food allergies.

Hospitals

If you have an accident and are taken to hospital against your wishes, you must contact your mentor as soon as possible. A vampire doctor will arrange for your removal to a private hospital where you can be treated appropriately.

Injury

You will recover more quickly and completely from injury than an NV.

Even so, you cannot regrow parts of your body that have been cut off, and serious injuries will leave scars.

You will feel the same level of pain when injured as an NV.

iVamp

The iVamp application will help you to keep in touch with other vampires and your mentor.

Please check your iVamp account at least once a day.

iVamp will be moved to smart phones soon.

Kissing

You may kiss vampires freely. If you want to kiss NVs, take an extra proVamp capsule first.

Love

If you fall in love with an NV, tell your mentor. You will get one-to-one advice on what to do. Don't be ashamed – it has happened to many of us.

Meat

Meat is a good source of blood if eaten raw or nearly raw.

You may eat any meat that is normally eaten in the area you are living, but please don't draw attention to yourself by eating inappropriate meats. A vampire in China may eat dogs; a vampire in Europe should not eat dogs. A vampire in Europe may eat cows; a vampire in India should not eat cows.

Mentor

Your mentor is your first contact for advice and help of any kind. Your mentor will put you in

touch with an expert if necessary. Your mentor
has been specially chosen to suit your personality
and circumstances.

NV

Non-vampire.

Organ donor

You must not donate organs under any
circumstances. Do not carry an organ donor card.

Pregnancy

If you become pregnant, or make someone pregnant, contact your mentor for advice immediately. Do not be embarrassed; rapid action is essential.

ProVamp

ProVamp capsules provide the iron you need and will prevent you craving blood. Take one capsule every day at the same time each day.

If you are exposed to blood, or feel you are likely to be exposed to blood, take an extra capsule.

Take a capsule before kissing an NV.

ProVamp will be delivered to you regularly but, if you feel there is any danger of your running out, contact your mentor.

Staking

Many NVs believe that vampires can be destroyed by staking. We can be killed by staking if it is done properly, but often it is not. If the stake does not pierce the right part of the heart, the vampire will live.

If you have been been staked and are able to do so, contact your mentor. A paramedic de-staking team will be sent to help you. DO NOT try to remove a stake yourself. If you can't get hold of your mentor, call the Helpline on the local number you have been given.

Teeth

NVs believe that all vampires have pointy canine teeth. Many vampires do, in fact, file their canines, just as many NVs pierce their ears, but it is a cosmetic alteration and not a result of the condition.

Some older vampires had their teeth filed years ago when they needed to feed on humans. Newer vampires sometimes file their teeth for show.

If you want to have your teeth filed, your mentor can suggest a local dentist who will perform the task. Do not ask an NV dentist to do this.

Wedding

Avoid weddings; the need to count the rice grains or confetti thrown leads to awkward situations.

Yakutsk

A city in Russia close to the vampire research centre.

You may be asked to attend Yakutsk for testing during the first twenty years of being a vampire. One in five new vampires is tested at Yakutsk. Selection is random.

Dealing with the NV World

When you first become a vampire, it will feel strange. You will probably continue to think like an NV for a while.

But you will quickly adapt to becoming a vampire, and will find it difficult to relate to NVs.

This is the point when you will need help learning how to deal with the NV world.

Your mentor

Very soon after you have been vamped, you will be appointed a mentor. Your mentor will be an established vampire – someone who has been a vampire for at least fifty years.

He or she will guide you through the early days, months and years of your new state, giving advice and support and making sure that you know how to behave.

Complaints and arbitration

We do not expect you to have any complaints. We have been doing this a lot longer than you have and our methods have been worked out over thousands of years to benefit vampire-kind.

There is no appeals procedure and no process for arbitration.

If you think you have been hard-done-by, you are adopting a selfish, modern attitude which is not appropriate to your new life.

So get over it.

The Science of Being a Vampire

Our scientists are working hard to discover the exact cause and nature of vampirism.

Some of our scientists have been in our laboratories in Central Europe and Russia for hundreds of years.

Their best explanation so far is that vampirism is caused by a virus. We can describe the effects, but we cannot explain exactly how they come about.

For the latest information on the science of vampirehood, please consult the pages under the Science tab on *www.vampiredawn.co.uk* (English language version).

Vampirism makes your blood better at carrying oxygen. We believe it changes the haemoglobin in blood in some way. You need extra iron to produce the enhanced haemoglobin, which is why you crave blood.

Because your blood is much better at carrying oxygen, you don't need to breathe as much now that you are a vampire.

An NV uses only a tiny fraction of the oxygen breathed in, but a vampire uses all of it. Another result is that your blood delivers oxygen more efficiently to your body, so your heart can beat much more slowly.

Vampire fact and fiction

In this section we look at some common beliefs about vampires.

You will probably be familiar with some of these already.

Vampires have no reflection or shadow

True? **No**

This is a lie, spread by vampires to make it easier to trick people.

'Look, I have a reflection – so I can't be a vampire.'

Vampires are afraid of garlic

True? **Sort of**

Vampires have a dangerous allergic reaction to garlic. If you eat garlic, your mouth and throat will swell up and you will be unable to breathe. It is similar to a nut allergy in NVs.

Vampires have pointy teeth

True?  Sometimes

Many vampires in the past had their teeth filed because it made biting people easier. A sharp bite that causes less pain and smaller wounds makes it easier for the vampire and victim to cover up what is happening.

Filed teeth do not regrow, so you will encounter many vampires with filed teeth.

Vampires must sleep in a coffin/with some earth from their grave

True? **No**

Long ago, vampires often did sleep in their graves, at least for a while, as it was convenient and well-hidden.

The need for earth from the grave is a myth of unknown origin.

Vampires can turn into bats

True? **No**

The belief probably comes from the common use of capes by vampires. Capes were normal dress for men and women in the eighteenth century and do not have any particular association with vampires.

However, it is easy to hide in a black cape, so many vampires carried on wearing capes when they were no longer fashionable.

Vampires are burned by a crucifix/cannot enter a church

True? **Sometimes**

Previously-Christian vampires have a strong aversion to a crucifix or other religious items, including holy water.

The part of the brain that deals with religion is affected by vampirism, causing a terrible fear that the vampire is displeasing to his or her god and will be punished.

If the feeling is very strong, touching a crucifix can produce physical effects. This is most common in people who were previously very religious, and so it is more common amongst older vampires.

Vampires who previously followed a religion other than Christianity fear symbols of their own religion.

Vampires cannot cross running water

True? 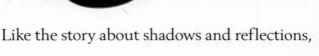 No

Like the story about shadows and reflections, this is a myth encouraged by vampires.

Vampires have to count things

True?  Yes

One effect vampirism has on the brain is *arithmomania*, the need to count things.

It has been exploited by people for hundreds of years to keep vampires away.

Vampires always wear dark clothes

True?  No

Many vampires choose to wear black clothes as it is easy to go unseen in the dark when wearing black clothes. But many vampires wear perfectly ordinary clothes.

Vampires have pale skin and black hair

True?  No

Vampires with white skin are paler than they were. Vampires with Asian skin look slightly paler. Black vampires look the same as they ever did.

Vampires have the same variety of hair colour as NVs.

Vampires live forever

True? **Unknown**

Of course, a vampire would not live after the end of the world, with no oxygen or blood.

But we do not know how long a vampire may live.

Most die of accidents or murder – there is plenty of time to have an accident if you live around 800 years.

Validated vampire ages do not exceed 850 years so far, but there are several vampires who claim to be older.

Vampire History

You don't need to read this part of the Handbook, but you might find it interesting.

The earliest reports of vampires come from Ancient Babylon, 4,000 years ago. Although Ishtar claims to have been born in Ancient Babylon, there is no evidence to support his claim.

Scientists at the Yakutsk research base are using DNA from Mr Ishtar and Babylonian remains to test his claim.

There are many reports of Greek and Roman vampires.

During the 1700s, a vampire purge swept across Europe. Many vampires were murdered, some horribly mutilated; it was the darkest chapter in our history.

Empress Marie Theresa of Austro-Hungary told her court doctor Gerard van Swieten to investigate. He travelled for a long time around Europe and finally reported back to her that vampires do not exist. The empress passed a law forbidding people to harm dead bodies to stop them becoming vampires.

Gerard van Swieten still lives in Austria.

During the French Revolution (1789-1799), many vampires were executed simply because they were rich and French. Most were not suspected of being vampires.

Joseph Ignace Guillotin invented the guillotine, which was used from 1792 as a kinder method of execution than the axe or the sword.

Joseph (known as Ignace) Guillotin currently lives in Hungary and Paris.

Vampire
FAQs

What if someone discovers I am a vampire?

You should try to make sure that people do not discover you are a vampire.

If someone suspects, your first response should be to ridicule them. Remember, most people do not believe in vampires. You may be able to convince them that they are being silly.

Your second response is to 'prove' you are not a vampire. For example, you have a shadow and a reflection. Most people believe vampires have neither.

In addition, you can cross flowing water and you can go out in daylight.

If they test you in a way you cannot deal with, such as scattering rice or cutting you, you will need to leave the situation as soon as possible. Then contact your mentor or the emergency helpline for security back-up and advice.

What if I fall in love?

It is better to have relationships only with other vampires, but we recognise this does not always happen.

If you fall in love with a non-vampire, and your relationship has lasted more than five years, you can apply to your mentor for permission to marry and/or reveal your vampirehood.

But remember – they will get old and die. You will not.

Why don't I bleed?

You do bleed, but more slowly than before.

Your body makes much more efficient use of the oxygen you breathe in and so your blood flows very slowly – it simply doesn't need to carry oxygen around your body at speed.

As a result, blood leaks out slowly if you are cut.

Can I eat birthday cake, take-away meals and vegetables?

In small quantities these will do you no harm.

You might vomit if you eat too much 'normal' food, but you will not suffer lasting harm.

It is often better to eat and be sick than to cause offence or suspicion by refusing food. You must be the judge.

Can I be 'cured'?

No – vampirehood is not reversible. But remember – it is a *condition*, not a disease. 'Cure' is not an appropriate word. Be proud of your vampirehood!

How long will I live?

If you are not killed in an accident or by an NV, you could live for at least 800 years. This depends on the age at which you were vamped, though. Someone vamped at 80 might live only 100 years more.

What if I don't want to be a vampire? Can I kill myself?

Suicide is not allowed.

It is very difficult to kill yourself, and the usual result of suicide attempts is that the vampire community has to support injured or unwell vampires for many hundreds of years.

Be considerate and courteous to the vampire community, and seek help with feelings of depression and denial.

The Vampire Dawn Series

Vampire Dawn is a fictional series based on the experiences of five teenagers who become vampires during an outdoor survival challenge in Hungary.

Many stories have been written about vampires. Some have even been made into films. However none of these stories is based on what really happens to vampires.

Vampire Dawn is different. These stories do not pretend that vampirism is supernatural. They are written by *someone who knows* what vampire life is really like.

Die Now or Live forever

Five teenagers camping in a forest in Hungary stumble across a dead body. That's scary enough – but what happens next is beyond scary.

The discovery triggers a terrifying descent into blood-lust and vampirism that leads them into an ancient underworld ruled by a French nobleman nearly 400 years old.

The Vampire Dawn story starts with this book. Read it first. Then you can read the other books in the series in any order.

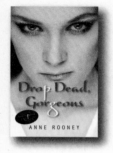

Drop Dead, Gorgeous

This is Juliette's story.

Juliette is a model – but she's also a vampire.

In the glamorous world of high fashion, her odd behaviour usually goes unnoticed. But a photo shoot in Paris brings Juliette face to face with how her life has changed since she became a vampire.

As she falls in love, she finds herself drawn into an alien world of passion, jealousy and murder that stretches back hundreds of years.

Life Sucks

This is Finn's story.

Finn's life sucks. And he writes songs about it. But now he's a vampire, he has something else to sing about, something unique – and dangerous. It adds an edge to his music that sees his career take off at last.

Fame and fortune are not that simple, though, and he soon finds that vampires make enemies easily.

Help comes from an unexpected source – but it's not going to be an easy ride.

Dead on Arrival

This is Ruby and Alistair's story.

What happens when a vampire is involved in a hit-and-run accident? And when the hospital where the body is taken is struck by a series of mysterious and ghastly crimes?

Ruby goes to the hospital to search for her vampire brother, Alistair, fearing the worst.

But his body has gone missing, and Ruby is soon caught in a tense life-or-death race to find out what has happened.

Every Drop of your Blood

This is Omar's story.

Omar thinks he's flying to New York for work experience in a laboratory – but he's kidnapped en route and taken far away.

With no possible way of escaping, he's forced to work with other vampires in a cutting-edge science establishment – but their methods are unorthodox and unethical, and he doesn't want to be involved.

Is Omar the experimenter – or is he the subject?

In Cold Blood

This is Ava's story.

Ava doesn't know how she came to be in Kosovo or what is wrong with her.

Released by the vampire elite, who believe she is immune to vampirism, she must fend for herself in the freezing Balkan winter.

When she falls for a boy who works in a circus, she thinks things are finally going her way – but terror is only ever one step behind her. From a fierce tiger to a famous murderer, she faces horror at every turn.

Vampire Dawn

Find out more at www.vampiredawn.co.uk. Follow the vampires
on Facebook: www.facebook.com/VampireDawnBooks
twitter: @vampiredawn

Remember:

One bite is all it takes...